T0197599

Dr. Vermeij's Conch Quest

written by
Fran Pollock Prezant
& Laura E. Marshak

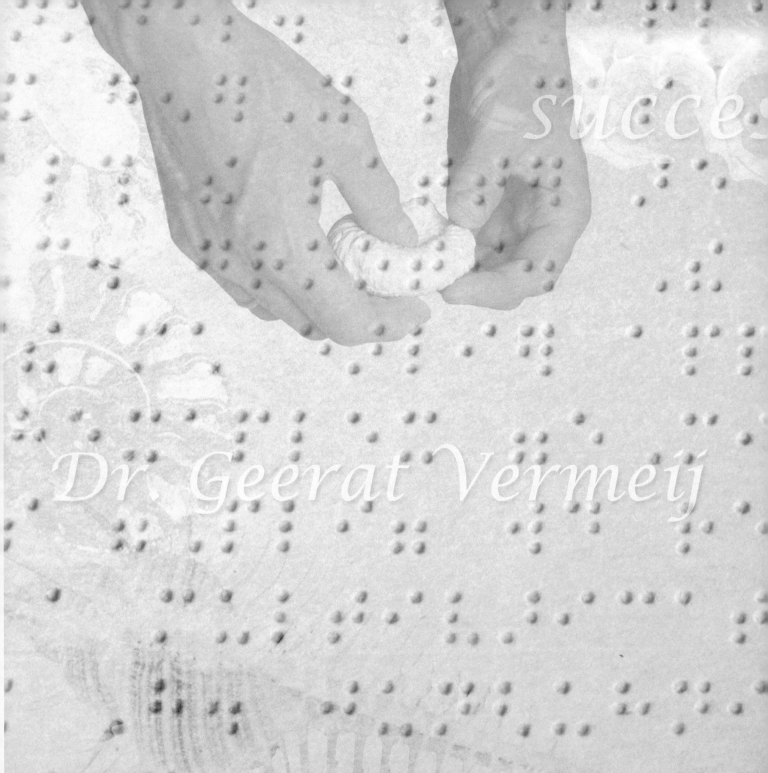

The authors would like to thank Dr. Geerat Vermeij for sharing his story. Dr. Vermeij is a Distinguished Professor in the Department of Geology at University of California at Davis. He has written and published over 100 scientific papers and several books including his autobiography, *Privileged Hands: A Scientific Life.* Dr. Vermeij has been awarded both MacArthur and Guggenheim fellowships. His wife, Edith Zipser, is also a biologist, and they have one daughter, Hermine.

The authors also thank Dr. Robert Prezant for critical review comments and nomenclature clarification.

Additionally, the authors gratefully acknowledge the contributions of Gerald McCormack of Cook Islands Natural Heritage Trust and Jim Stewart at the Zymoglyphic Museum.

This book was made possible in part by a USRC grant from Indiana University of Pennsylvania.

An accessible version of this book is available for individuals with qualified print disabilities through Bookshare. www.bookshare.org

AuthorHouse™
1663 Liberty Drive
Bloomington, IN 47403
www.authorhouse.com
Phone: 833-262-8899

Because of the dynamic nature of the Internet, any web addresses or links contained in this book may have changed since publication and may no longer be valid. The views expressed in this work are solely those of the author and do not necessarily reflect the views of the publisher, and the publisher hereby disclaims any responsibility for them.

This book is printed on acid-free paper.

ISBN: 978-1-4490-9199-6 (sc)
       978-1-4772-2482-3 (e)

Library of Congress Control Number: 2010923926

Print information available on the last page.

Published by AuthorHouse 03/02/2021

authorHOUSE®

Dr. Vermeij's Conch Quest

Fran Pollock Prezant

Laura E. Marshak

design, typography, and layout by Danielle L. Wolfe

The authors would like to dedicate this book to all of the parents, educators, and other professionals who identify and stimulate interests in young children, see possibilities, and proactively take opportunities to foster positive career outcomes for all students.

Can you imagine floating for your whole life on a raft of bubbles? This beautiful violet snail does just that and even blows its own bubbles! It bobs like an upside down top in the ocean. It never touches sand or shore. The shell has two colors. If you were in a boat and looked down at the snail, it would look dark violet like the ocean. If you were swimming under the water and looked up at the snail, it would look light blue like the sky. How could its colors protect the snail?

This unusual snail adds pebbles and shells to itself as it moves. It is like a walking sculpture that keeps changing. It puts its foot down, raises its shell, and throws itself forward to move. This is called a one-legged stomp or *galumphing*. Why do you think it is called the Carrier shell? Do you think that the things it collects make it stronger? Do they help it to hide? Do they keep it from flipping over? Why is this important?

The shell of this snail looks like a delicate comb. The long white spines look fragile enough to break. They belong to the Venus comb murex. Why do you think this animal has such an unusual shape? What do you think its spines do?

The violet snail, the Carrier shell and the Venus comb murex are types of animals called molluscs. The scientist, Dr. Geerat Vermeij, studies molluscs. Because he lost his vision as a young child and could not see, he felt the shells with his fingers. Geerat had many questions about the shells he touched. Why did some have lots of ridges and whorls but others did not? Why did some feel chalky, yet others felt smooth like glass? His fourth grade teacher encouraged his interest through her stories of shells in faraway places. She also started a shell collection on the classroom windowsill.

As Geerat felt the shells with his fingers, he dreamed about the tropical seas where some of them once lived. He thought about sandy beaches, palm trees, and warm sparkling waters. When he grew up, he became a scientist and traveled to the misty shores of Peru and to the cold, rocky Aleutian Islands. Geerat went to these places to unlock the secrets of molluscs, but it all began as a child with his close observations, thoughts about what he noticed, and questions that came from his observations. Finding answers to these questions became a fun goal. It was like finding a key to a locked gate or unwrapping a surprise gift.

All plants and animals have common names

like man, cat, or dog. They also have scientific names like *Homo sapien*, *Felis catus*, or *Canis familiaris*. When a new type of animal is identified, the person who discovered it gives it a name. This process has certain rules so that people worldwide use the same name to talk about the same animal. Scientists have named new species because of the way they look, what they do, where they were found, or in honor of a person. *Editharus angulilabris* is a mollusc that Geerat named after his wife, Edith. Some biological names are very short, like the spider named *Oops*. Some are very long like the sea urchin named *Stongelocentrotus droebachiensis*. Some are funny, like the snails named *Ba humbugi* and *Abra cadabra!*

Geerat liked the Latin names of the shells. Names

like *Strombus* and *Terebra* sounded exotic. He was curious about the common names of shells too. He enjoyed thinking about names like helmet shell, snakeskin turban, green volcano, swollen olive, soldier cone, tusk shell, and pen shell. Why do you think these shells were given these common names?

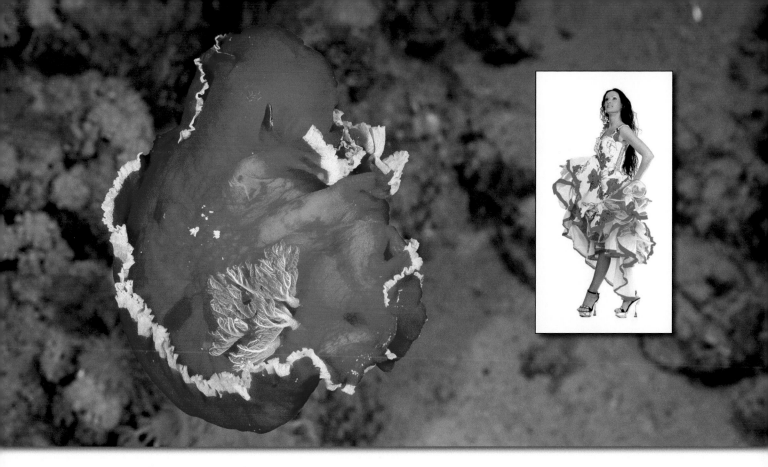

Geerat learned that these shells were part of a large group of creatures called molluscs. The word *mollusc* means *soft*. These animals have soft bodies. Many have shells that we can see. Some have shells buried under their skin. Some have no shells at all. Molluscs include clams, oysters, snails, slugs, octopuses, and squids. Molluscs also include colorful nudibranchs. These are sea slugs or naked snails. This one is called the Spanish dancer. Use your imagination.

Molluscs come in many sizes. The giant clam is the largest mollusc with an external shell. It can measure 4 feet and weigh 500 pounds! It is so large that a child can fit inside it! Some other clams are so small that you could barely see one on your fingertip. There are snails that are longer than 2 feet. Some snails are so small that 50 of them side by side would only measure one inch long! There are over 100,000 kinds of molluscs that have been identified. Scientists name

400-500 new ones each year. Many molluscs are still waiting to be found. Some are in exotic places. Many can be close to your home in the ocean, in lakes and rivers, on land, and in trees.

Molluscs can be very different from each other. Some cone snails from Australia are among the most poisonous animals in the world. They inject their prey with venom. They inject it with a hollow tooth, like a dart. They catch small fish and worms this way. There is also the beautiful trumpet snail. Its shell can be played like a trumpet. It is used as a foghorn or a warning call. Some people in Hawaii and the Pacific Islands blow it to celebrate the daily sunset. There is even a clam that looks like a worm and eats wood!

Geerat learned that if he became a scientist, he could study molluscs and find answers to his questions. His parents encouraged his curiosity. They helped Geerat to be a good observer by describing to him everything that he could not see. His brother, Arie, created raised pictures of shells for Geerat to feel.

Some people doubted that someone who is blind could be a scientist. They wondered how he could do what scientists do. They thought his world was dark. Geerat did not know why they thought this. He described the world around him as sparkling with sounds, smells, shapes, and textures. Geerat was a happy boy who found the world fascinating.

Today, *Geerat is known as Dr. Vermeij*, a successful malacologist. This is a scientist who studies molluscs. He is also a college professor. He shares his research on molluscs in speeches, articles, and books. Some of his books have even been printed in other languages such as Japanese.

Reading is a very important part of Geerat's work. He knows that science is not just about making observations. You need to read about other people's ideas and discoveries. He has been an eager reader since he was a boy. He learned to read Braille when he was young. This is how he reads today. Braille is a series of raised dots that represent letters and numbers. People who learn Braille feel these dots with their fingertips as a method of reading.

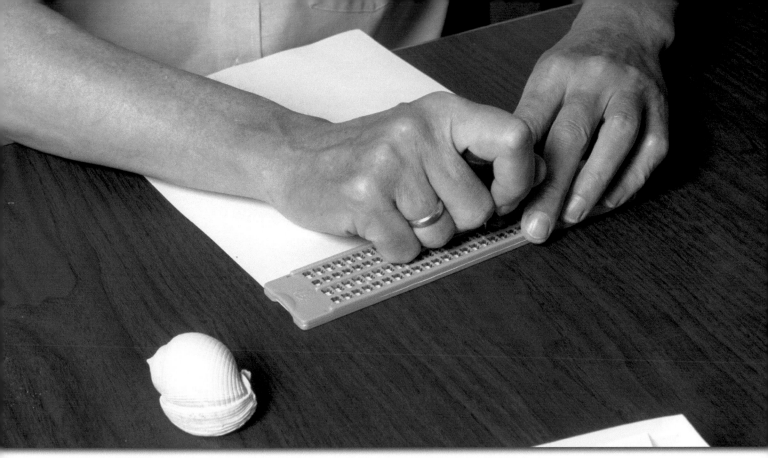

Geerat has a huge library of Braille books, articles, reports, and his own notes. He writes in Braille using a device that produces the raised dots on paper. He also uses a Braille typewriter. Sometimes other people read to him. This is for convenience only. He is able to read Braille English, French, German, Spanish, and Dutch.

Geerat has collected thousands of molluscs from all over the world. One of his favorite places to study is the Palau Islands. He describes Palau as a mix of rainforests and rocky coral reefs. There are palm trees along the shore. The water is warm and calm. He also loves the island of Guam. He describes it as "love at first feel". It has warm, moist air, sweet smelling plants, and the sound of cackling geckos. The waves sound like thunder when they crash on the shore. The coast is full of large, slippery rocks. Moray eels and crabs hide inside the deep holes of these rocks.

Geerat works with many types of molluscs and sea creatures. He collects these animals using all of his senses-except vision. He wades in the water carefully. He feels under the rocks and sifts through sand and mud. He finds clams by feeling tiny bursts of water under his feet. He finds snapping shrimp by listening for the "popping" sounds that they make as they close their claws. He can often smell sponges and then use his fingers to find them. His fingers also help him to identify the smooth round bodies of sea anemones.

He gently touches and identifies creatures but does so quickly. Why? He must stay alert for dangers such as moray eels, stingrays, nipping crabs, and large waves. That's why. He knows he is taking some risks. Some people think that if you are blind, you must avoid all risks. Geerat knows this is not true.

When he brings the creatures back to his laboratory, Geerat studies them closely. He checks their shapes, sizes, and weights. He uses special tools to test their openings and hinges. Most scientists use their sight to inspect an animal. Geerat uses his sense of touch to "see" the shape, size, weight, and texture of the specimen. His hands are the best tools that he has to examine molluscs. He can even feel scars on the shells. Scars could tell him that the animal was damaged or attacked during its life. Geerat runs his fingernails over the shells. He finds patterns in textures that vision alone could miss. Sometimes he drags a needle inside the shell openings. This causes vibrations as the needle hits ridges and grooves. This provides a unique source of information too. He also measures shells with calipers. When he measures shells with calipers, he can feel the dial to learn the size of the shells.

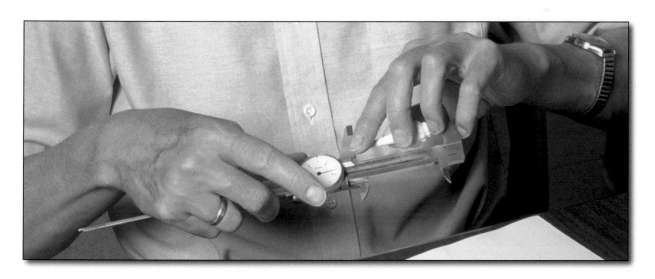

Geerat believes that studying shells and molluscs is one way to understand more about how life works and has changed over time. There are many questions. Why are shells that live in cold water different than shells that live in warm water? Why do molluscs that live in the deep sea have such thin shells? Why do most mollusc shells have spirals?

Most molluscs actually make their own home, the shell, and it also part of them. Geerat is curious about the shape and the texture of shells. He believes that shells can tell how molluscs have adapted to survive their world.

Periwinkle snails are found along many coasts. These snails are a good example of how small molluscs survive. Like many other snails, they glide slowly on one big foot. It does not look like your foot. They can pull their foot up into their shells. Then they seal themselves inside with a trap door called an operculum. This protects it from predators, the heat, and dryness outside. Some land snails also make mucus that helps it stick onto things and prevents it from drying out.

Learning about molluscs that are alive today made Geerat want to know more about molluscs of the past. He began to study fossils. Fossils are the remains of plants or animals. This includes their ancient shells. Have you ever picked up a rock and found in it what looked like the imprint of an animal or shell? That may have been a fossil. The oldest molluscs lived about 530 million years ago. Geerat is known for his study of the relationship between predator and prey, like crabs and molluscs. He does this by looking at how shells have changed over time. These changes protect the shell owners from attackers like crabs, fish, and bigger molluscs.

Curiosity makes a good scientist. In fact, it was the beginning of Geerat's success. He always questioned things, even the familiar aspects of his world. To be a scientist, you need to work hard. The abilities to observe, think, and read are very important. Think extra hard about things that puzzle you. Puzzles and mysteries lead to important questions, and questions are the beginning of new discoveries.

Fran Prezant is a Senior Vice President at Abilities!, a nonprofit organization in New York. She can be reached at fprezant@abilitiesonline.org.

Laura Marshak is a Professor of Counselor Education at the Indiana University of Pennsylvania and a practicing psychologist in Pittsburgh, PA. She can be reached at marshak@iup.edu.

This is the fourth book thay have co-authored together.

Printed in the United States
by Baker & Taylor Publisher Services